12:37

Julia Pascal

LONDON • NEW YORK • OXFORD • NEW DELHI • SYDNEY

METHUEN DRAMA
Bloomsbury Publishing Plc
50 Bedford Square, London, WC1B 3DP, UK
1385 Broadway, New York, NY 10018, USA
29 Earlsfort Terrace, Dublin 2, Ireland

BLOOMSBURY, METHUEN DRAMA and the Methuen
Drama logo are trademarks of Bloomsbury Publishing Plc

First published in Great Britain 2022

A catalogue record for this book is available from the British Library.

A catalog record for this book is available from the Library of Congress.

ISBN: PB: 978-1-3503-8054-7
ePDF: 978-1-3503-8055-4
eBook: 978-1-3503-8056-1

Series: Modern Plays

Typeset by Mark Heslington Ltd, Scarborough, North Yorkshire

To find out more about our authors and books visit
www.bloomsbury.com and sign up for our newsletters.

Pascal Theatre Company
in association with
Neil McPherson for the Finborough Theatre
presents

The world premiere

12:37

Written and Directed by Julia Pascal

First performance at the Finborough Theatre:
Tuesday, 29 November 2022

This production is supported by

 The Royal Victoria
Hall Foundation

12:37

by Julia Pascal

Cast in order of appearance

Paul Green	**Alex Cartuson**
Eileen O'Reilly	**Lisa O'Connor**
Rina Goldberg	**Lisa O'Connor**
Cecil Green	**Eoin O'Dubhghaill**
Minnie (Naomi) Green	**Ruth Lass**
Shoshana Liebovicz	**Ruth Lass**
Matron	**Ruth Lass**
Harry Cohen	**Danann McAleer**
Jonathan Stein	**Danann McAleer**
British Soldiers and Generals	**Danann McAleer**

Other roles played by members of the company.

Dublin 1935, London 1936 and Palestine 1946.

The performance lasts approximately two hours including the interval.

There will be one interval of fifteen minutes.

Director	**Julia Pascal**
Set and Costume Designer	**Liberty Monroe**
Lighting Designer	**Jon Stacey**
Sound Designer	**Flick Isaac-Chilton**
Assistant Director and Stage Manager	**Anastasia Bunce**
Executive Producer	**Susannah Levene**

PLEASE BE CONSIDERATE OF OTHERS. WE RECOMMEND WEARING A FACE COVERING FULLY COVERING YOUR MOUTH AND NOSE FOR THE DURATION OF THE PERFORMANCE.

MASKS ARE MANDATORY ON SUNDAY MATINEE PERFORMANCES.

Please see front of house notices or ask an usher for an exact running time.

Please turn your mobile phones off – the light they emit can also be distracting.

Alex Cartuson | Paul Green

Theatre includes *Eureka Day* (Old Vic), *My Friend Peter* (Arts Theatre), *War Horse* (national and international tour), *The Importance of Being Earnest* (UK tour) and *Richard III* (UK and France tour).

Film includes *Being Brunel* and *The Crime*.

Television includes *The Moment* and the Birmingham Commonwealth Games Opening Ceremony.

Ruth Lass | Minnie (Naomi) Green, Shoshana Liebovicz, Matron

Productions at the Finborough Theatre include *The Hospital at the Time of the Revolution*.

Trained at the Royal Academy of Dramatic Art.

Theatre includes *Bach and Sons* (Bridge Theatre), *Crooked Dances* (The Other Place), *Equus* (Theatre Royal Stratford East and UK tour), *Great Apes* (Arcola Theatre), *A Short History of Tractors in Ukrainian* (Hull Truck Theatre), *The Rest Is Silence* (Riverside Studios and World Shakespeare Festival), *Wagner Dream* and *The Tempest* (Barbican Theatre), *Hamlet* (Riverside Studios), *The Girl on the Sofa* (Royal Lyceum Theatre, Edinburgh, as part of Edinburgh International Festival), *Martin Yesterday* (Royal Exchange Theatre, Manchester), *The House of Bernarda Alba* (Young Vic), *Uganda* and *Live Like Pigs* (Royal Court Theatre), *The Skryker* (National Theatre), *Hurricane Roses* and *Uganda* (National Theatre Studio), *Les Justes* and *Hecuba* (Gate Theatre), *Mrs Klein* (Watford Palace Theatre), *And All Because the Lady Loves* (Soho Theatre) and *The Dybbuk* (New End Theatre and international tour).

Film includes *Disobedience*, *The Book of Gabrielle*, *Mad Cows*, *Fill Up* and *Indian Summer*.

Television includes *C.B. Strike – Lethal White*, *Silent Witness*, *Houdini and Doyle*, *EastEnders*, *White Teeth*, *Holby City*, *Coupling*, *High Stakes*, *Trial and Retribution*, *Antigone*, *Casualty* and *The Bill*.

Danann McAleer | Harry Cohen, Jonathan Stein

Trained at Bristol Old Vic Theatre School.

Theatre includes *Dr Semmelweis* (Bristol Old Vic), *The Hamlet Voyage* (Bridewell Theatre), *Richard II* (The Vaults and Turbine Theatre), *Under The Greenwood Tree* (Everyman Theatre, Cheltenham), *A Midsummer Night's Dream* and *Our Country's Good* (Tobacco Factory, Bristol), *King Lear* (Bristol Old Vic), *Frankenstein* (Arnos Vale Cemetery, Bristol), *Penny Dreadful* (Arts Mansion, Bristol), *The Comedy of Errors* and *The Tempest* (international tour) and *Don Quixote* (Wigmore Hall).

Film includes *Is That All There Is?*, *Living in Crime Alley*, *Seven Days that Made the Führer*, *Conversations with Strangers* and *Watch Over Me*.

Lisa O'Connor | Eileen O'Reilly, Rina Goldberg

Trained at Cork School of Music.

Theatre whilst training includes *Medea Redux* and *Blood Wedding* (Cork School of Music) and *Epic Stages* (National Youth Theatre).

Theatre includes *This Is a Blizzard* (National Tour).

Television includes *Call the Midwife*.

Lisa was a winner of Monologue Slam UK National Finals in 2018.

Eoin O'Dubhghaill | Cecil Green

Theatre includes *Sruth Na Teanga* (Branar), *Nóra* and *Song of the Yellow Bittern* (An Taibhdhearc), and *Dear Ireland – End Meeting* and *Baoite* (Abbey Theatre, Dublin).

Film and television includes *Harry Wild, Arracht, Ros na Rún, Out of Innocence* and *Grace Harte*.

Eoin is also an accomplished singer and musician, who plays multiple instruments, including guitar, tin whistle and bodhrán. He is a native Irish-language speaker.

Julia Pascal | Playwright and Director

Productions at the Finborough Theatre include *Blueprint Medea* which also won the Dan I Rodden Jr Play Award.

Julia trained at E15 Acting School and worked as a stage, television and screen actor before coming to public attention as the first woman director at the National Theatre with *Men Seldom Make Passes*. This was her adaptation of Dorothy Parker's writings, which ran for two years as a Platform Performance. She has directed dramas by Seamus Finnegan, Carole Rumens and Miryam Sivan. Her productions include Harold Pinter's *The Caretaker* for the British Council and Bertolt Brecht's *Man Is Man* for RADA. As Associate Director of the Orange Tree Theatre, Richmond, she directed texts by Alfonso Vallejo, Howard Brenton, Bertolt Brecht and Fay Weldon.

Her plays have been seen in France, Germany, Austria, Liechtenstein, Ireland and in New York City, at the Lincoln Center's Directors Lab and at Theatre for the New City. Texts include *The Holocaust Trilogy – Theresa, A Dead Woman on Holiday* and *The Dybbuk* (New End Theatre and European tour), *The Yiddish Queen Lear* (Southwark Playhouse), *Woman in the Moon* (Arcola Theatre), *The Golem* (Purcell Room), *St Joan* (New End Theatre, Paris and Edinburgh Festival), *Year Zero* (Maubeuge, France, and The Junction, Cambridge), *The Shylock Play* (Arcola Theatre), *Honeypot* (New Diorama Theatre), *Nineveh* (Riverside Studios), her adaptation of Charlotte Brontë's novel *Villette* (The British Library), *Crossing Jerusalem*, commissioned by the Tricycle Theatre (Tricycle Theatre and Park Theatre) and *Old Newland*, commissioned and produced by Theatre Delicatessen. For the Bloomsbury Festival, she has written, directed and produced two site-specific performances. *Dancing, Talking, Taboo* (St Pancras Church) and *Dancing, Trailblazing, Taboo! Eleanor Marx, A Life in Movement* (Royal National Hotel). She has written and presented the documentary *The Crime That Only Women Commit* (BBC World Service). At the University of York and at the Wiener Holocaust Library she was Writer in Residence. Her scripts are published by Oberon Books, Bloomsbury, Faber and Virago.

Julia's many awards include a BBC Alfred Bradley Prize for *Theresa* and the radio version was nominated for the Sony Prize. She received a National Endowment for Science, Technology and the Arts (NESTA) Fellowship and grants from the Arts Council, the European Association for Jewish Culture, the Jewish Historical Society of England, the Leverhulme Trust, The Moondance Columbine Award for *Crossing Jerusalem*, the Oppenheim–John Downes Memorial Trust and the Goethe-Institut. She was awarded her PhD from the University of York in 2016 and is currently a Research Fellow at King's College, University of London.

Julia's next play, *As Happy as God in France*, explores a meeting between Hannah Arendt and Charlotte Salomon in a French internment camp during 1940. It will have a staged reading for Holocaust Memorial Day at Burgh House, Hampstead, on 26 January 2023. Her play *A Manchester Girlhood* will be seen in Manchester and Blackpool in April 2023. Pascal Theatre Company is currently funded by the Lottery Heritage Fund for the project *Women for Women: Bloomsbury 1800–1900*.

www.pascal-theatre.com

Liberty Monroe | Set and Costume Design

Trained at RADA.

Designs includes *East End Masculinities* (Voicebox Theatre), *The Faith Machine* (George Bernard Shaw Theatre) and *When the Rain Stops Falling* (Vanbrugh Theatre).

Jon Stacey | Lighting Design

Lighting design includes *Lillies on the Land* (National Tour), *Khojaly* (St Paul's Church, Covent Garden, and Union Theatre), *Addams Family* (Waterside Theatre, Aylesbury), *Spring Awakening*, *Rent* and *Carrie* (Frogmore Paper Mill), *Frankenstein* and *Dracula* (The Spire, Brighton), *Hourglass*, *Cry Baby*, *Songs for a New World* and *Our House* (University of Chichester) and *Rent* (International College of Musical Theatre).

Flick Isaac-Chilton | Sound Design

Sound design and composition includes *Meat Cute* (Chiswick Playhouse), *I Am Turpin* and *Salomé* (Theatre N16), *A Little Princess* (Edinburgh Festival) and *And Eve?* and *[redacted]* (Catalyst in the Cloud).

Flick is also a musician who has performed at the Shaftesbury, Savoy and Adelphi Theatres, the Royal Albert Hall, Barbican, Arcola Theatre, Southwark Playhouse, Soho Theatre, The Other Palace and ATG Aylesbury Waterside, and has recorded for Broadway on Demand.

Anastasia Bunce | Assistant Director and Stage Manager

Productions at the Finborough Theatre include assistant director on *Not Quite Jerusalem* and directing *Darkie Armo Girl*.

Stage management includes *The Kind Refuser* (Omnibus Theatre).

Directing includes *Blood on Your Hands* (Cockpit Theatre) and *Meat Cute* (Bread and Roses Theatre, Chiswick Playhouse and Hen and Chickens Theatre).

Anastasia runs new writing company Patch Plays which stages work exploring animal ethics and sustainability.

Susannah Levene | Executive Producer

Susannah began her career acting in pantomime, fringe, commercial theatre and repertory theatre before changing direction and becoming a residential social worker. She returned to theatre in general management where she has run venues from the Lyceum Theatre, Crewe, to the Studio Theatre at the Theatre Museum.

She has been General Manager/Producer for companies including Clean Break, Sphinx, Yellow Earth Theatre, Pascal Theatre Company and the Mama Quilla Initiative, and most recently worked with Trafalgar Entertainment.

She has been a mentor for dancers through One Dance UK and is a frequent guest lecturer at E15 Acting School. She is Trustee and Chair of Sphinx Theatre Company, and Producer and Management Consultant for Pascal Theatre Company.

Production Acknowledgements

Photography	**Yaron Lapid**
Press Representative	**Rebecca Bullamore at Kate Morley PR**

With special thanks to cellist Natalie Clein for kind permission to use her interpretation of *Kol Nidre*, Peter Silverleaf for voice recordings, David Schneider for Yiddish translation, Chazan Shalom Rapoport for cantorial training, Andrea Nouryeh for dramaturgical input, Ruth Posner and Kasia Moravka for Polish consultancy, Lesley Lightfoot for costumes and King's College, London for space.

FINBOROUGH THEATRE

"**Probably the most influential fringe theatre in the world.**" *Time Out*

"**Not just a theatre, but a miracle.**" *Metro*

"**The mighty little Finborough which, under Neil McPherson, continues to offer a mixture of neglected classics and new writing in a cannily curated mix.**" Lyn Gardner, *The Stage*

"**The tiny but mighty Finborough**" Ben Brantley, *The New York Times*

Founded in 1980, the multi-award-winning Finborough Theatre presents plays and music theatre, concentrated exclusively on vibrant new writing and unique rediscoveries from the 19th and 20th centuries, both in our 154-year-old home and online with our #FinboroughFrontier digital initiative.

Our programme is unique – we never present work that has been seen anywhere in London during the last 25 years. Behind the scenes, we continue to discover and develop a new generation of theatre makers.

Despite remaining completely unsubsidised, the Finborough Theatre has an unparalleled track record for attracting the finest talent who go on to become leading voices in British theatre. Under Artistic Director Neil McPherson, it has discovered some of the UK's most exciting new playwrights including Laura Wade, James Graham, Mike Bartlett, Jack Thorne, Nicholas de Jongh and Anders Lustgarten, and directors including Tamara Harvey, Caitriona McLaughlin, Robert Hastie, Blanche McIntyre, Kate Wasserberg and Sam Yates.

Artists working at the theatre in the 1980s included Clive Barker, Rory Bremner, Nica Burns, Kathy Burke, Ken Campbell, Jane Horrocks, Nicola Walker and Claire Dowie. In the 1990s, the Finborough Theatre first became known for new writing including Naomi Wallace's first play *The War Boys*, Rachel Weisz in David Farr's *Neville Southall's Washbag*, four plays by Anthony Neilson including *Penetrator* and *The Censor*, both of which transferred to the Royal Court Theatre, and new plays by Richard

Bean, Lucinda Coxon, David Eldridge and Tony Marchant. New writing development included the premieres of modern classics such as Mark Ravenhill's *Shopping and F**king*, Conor McPherson's *This Lime Tree Bower*, Naomi Wallace's *Slaughter City* and Martin McDonagh's *The Pillowman*.

Since 2000, new British plays have included Laura Wade's London debut *Young Emma*, commissioned for the Finborough Theatre, James Graham's *Albert's Boy* with Victor Spinetti, Sarah Grochala's *S27*, Athena Stevens' *Schism* which was nominated for an Olivier Award, and West End transfers for Joy Wilkinson's *Fair*, Nicholas de Jongh's *Plague Over England*, Jack Thorne's *Fanny and Faggot*, Neil McPherson's Olivier Award nominated *It Is Easy to Be Dead* and Dawn King's *Foxfinder*.

UK premieres of foreign plays have included plays by Brad Fraser, Lanford Wilson, Larry Kramer, Tennessee Williams, Suzan-Lori Parks, Jordan Tannahill, the English premieres of two Scots-language classics by Robert McLellan, and West End transfers for Frank McGuinness's *Gates of Gold* with William Gaunt and John Bennett, and Craig Higginson's *Dream of the Dog* with Dame Janet Suzman.

Rediscoveries of neglected work – most commissioned by the Finborough Theatre – have included the first London revivals of Rolf Hochhuth's *Soldiers* and *The Representative*, both parts of Keith Dewhurst's *Lark Rise to Candleford*, *Etta Jenks* with Clarke Peters and Daniela Nardini, Noël Coward's first play *The Rat Trap*, and Lennox Robinson's *Drama at Inish* with Celia Imrie and Paul O'Grady. Emlyn Williams's *Accolade* and John Van Druten's *London Wall* both transferred to St James' Theatre, whilst J. B. Priestley's *Cornelius* transferred to a sell-out Off Broadway run in New York City.

Music theatre has included the new (premieres from Craig Adams, Grant Olding, Charles Miller, Michael John LaChuisa, Adam Guettel, Andrew Lippa, Paul Scott Goodman, Polly Pen, and Adam Gwon's *Ordinary Days* which transferred to the West End) and the old (the UK premiere of Rodgers and Hammerstein's *State Fair* which also transferred to the West End), and the acclaimed 'Celebrating British Music Theatre' series.

The Finborough Theatre won the 2020 London Pub Theatres Pub Theatre of the Year Award, *The Stage* Fringe Theatre of the Year Award in 2011, the Empty Space Peter Brook Award in both 2010 and 2012, and was nominated for an Olivier Award in 2017 and 2019. Artistic Director Neil McPherson was awarded the Critics' Circle Special Award for Services to Theatre in 2019. It is the only unsubsidised theatre ever to be awarded the Channel 4 Playwrights Scheme bursary eleven times.

www.finboroughtheatre.co.uk

FINBOROUGH THEATRE

118 Finborough Road, London SW10 9ED
admin@finboroughtheatre.co.uk
www.finboroughtheatre.co.uk

The Finborough Theatre is a member of the Independent Theatre
Council, the Society of Independent Theatres, Musical Theatre Network,
The Friends of Brompton Cemetery, The Earl's Court Society,
The Kensington Society, and supports #time4change's
Mental Health Charter.

Supported by

The Earls Court Development Company

Theatres Trust

THE CARNE TRUST
Supporting young talent in the performing arts

Mailing

Email admin@finboroughtheatre.co.uk or give your details to our Box Office staff to join our free email list.

Playscripts

Many of the Finborough Theatre's plays have been published and are on sale from our website.

Environment

The Finborough Theatre has a 100% sustainable electricity supply.

Local History

The Finborough Theatre's local history website is online at
www.earlscourtlocalhistory.co.uk

On Social Media

 www.facebook.com/FinboroughTheatre

 www.twitter.com/finborough

 www.instagram.com/finboroughtheatre

 www.youtube.com/user/finboroughtheatre

 https://www.tiktok.com/@finboroughtheatre

Friends

The Finborough Theatre is a registered charity. We receive no public funding, and rely solely on the support of our audiences. Please do consider supporting us by becoming a member of our Friends of the Finborough Theatre scheme. There are four categories of Friends, each offering a wide range of benefits.

Smoking is not permitted in the auditorium.
The videotaping or making of electronic or other audio and/or visual recordings or streams of this production is strictly prohibited.

In accordance with the requirements of the Royal Borough of Kensington and Chelsea:
1. The public may leave at the end of the performance by all doors and such doors must at that time be kept open.
2. All gangways, corridors, staircases and external passageways intended for exit shall be left entirely free from obstruction whether permanent or temporary.
3. Persons shall not be permitted to stand or sit in any of the gangways intercepting the seating or to sit in any of the other gangways.

The Finborough Theatre is a registered charity and a company limited by guarantee. Registered in England and Wales no. 03448268. Registered Charity no. 1071304. Registered Office: 118 Finborough Road, London SW10 9ED.

12:37

PREFACE
Julia Pascal

WHY WRITE THIS PLAY NOW?

Is this a good time to be writing about Jews blowing up the British?
asks a Jewish colleague. I understand the anxiety behind her
question. More than half of the UK population holds
antisemitic views according to recent surveys. The last thing
the tiny British Jewish community wants is a play that shows
a Jewish history of violence against the British Army.

AN UNCOMFORTABLE HISTORY

British Jews have traditionally kept a very low profile.
Memories of murder and deportation from English soil
remain in our collective memory. The royal edit of 1290 was
Europe's first explusion of Jews, an act has never been
cancelled. British Jews also know that English literature is
full of antisemitic stereotypes. And in living memory there
are still witnesses to the annihilation of Jews in the Shoah.

And despite this background, yes I am writing a play that
reveals an uncomfortable history.

IRISH, JEWISH, INDIAN CONNECTIONS

12:37 connects the intersected twentieth-century nationalist
struggles of Irish, Indian and Jewish nationalists. Each fought
British occupation; a link I thought it important to highlight.

INTERVIEWING THE ACTIVISTS

The history behind the narrative of this epic was inspired by
interviewing Jewish activists. Of particular importance was
the testament of Hungarian-born Kariel Gardosche, known
in Israel as the cartoonist Dosh. As a prisoner Dosh escaped
the Nazis and fought with the Yugoslav partisans. He arrived
illegally into Palestine where he painted anti-British posters.
For this he was imprisoned in Acre jail. Others I interviewed,
British-born Jews, made me promise never to reveal their
names. They were scared of retribution, even decades after
the establishment of the state of Israel. These Jews were not

religious. They were inspired by the lives of Michael Collins and Pundit Nehru. Consideration about others, who also felt that Palestine was theirs, was submerged in their urgency to get the Brits out.

JEWISH WOMEN'S HIDDEN HISTORIES

Rina is an example of a vibrant Yiddish theatre that I discovered in the work of Luba Kadison and Molly Picon. She expresses a Jewish, transgressional culture that has now been largely absorbed into the mainstream, particularly in US cinema. It was important to me to reveal female agency within this specific artistic and political environment. But the text also addresses a particular 'reluctant history'. Little has been written about sexual abuse against Jewish women during the Shoah, whereas testimony is now surfacing about the occupation of Korea and China and how the Japanese army forced women into sexual slavery. In *12:37*, the development of Rina's character, from champion of the Soviet dream to right-wing political activist, is provoked by what happens to her in the Shoah.

WHERE JAMES JOYCE COMES INTO THIS

As for the protagonists, Paul and Cecil Green, their voices are rooted in a Joycean, Jewish Dublin which I heard in my own family. My father and his brothers were socialists who graduated as doctors in Dublin. Unlike Paul and Cecil, they were followers of Ben Gurion. I allowed myself to imagine what might have happened had they moved to the right. Joyce was no nationalist and his flight from it is close to that of the diaspora Jew. Joyce, of course, knew nothing of the Shoah or how the Jewish experience was utterly changed by it.

JEWISH ARCHETYPES AND STEREOTYPES

Within the dramatic journeys made by Cecil, Paul and Rina is the ongoing conflict between the archetype of the Jew as Healer or Jew as Warrior. This text aims to address the complexity of nationalism within the many Jewish voices in Britain and internationally. The history may be painful for British Jews but it should not be forgotten.

James Joyce saw that The Jew was the real protagonist of modern history. Joyce knew nothing of the Holocaust, of course, but he did recognise that The Jew was the key figure of modern history. Not the Christian. Not the pagan. In modern life. And of course in Modern Literature.

Anthony Burgess

Characters

Minnie (Naomi) Green, *Irish, Jewish, working class, fifty*
Paul Green, *oldest son, twenty-four*
Cecil Green, *youngest son, twenty-three*
Eileen O'Reilly, *Paul's girlfriend, Irish, Catholic, twenty-five*
Harry Cohen, *boxing trainer, London, working-class Jewish, fifty*
Rina Goldberg, *Lithuanian-born, Yiddish actor, twenty-five*
Jonathan Stein, *English conservative, middle-class Jew, fifty*
Shoshana Liebovicz, *Zionist activist, any age*
Matron in the London Hospital, *any age*
Ensemble

The first production uses a cast of five with the following multi-casting:
Minnie/Shoshana/Matron
Harry/Jonathan/Oswald Mosley/British Army Officer
Eileen/Rina
Paul/Wedding Guest
Cecil/British Army soldiers

Prologue

A Dublin Street

Spotlight upstage centre.

Paul *is holding* **Eileen**. *He is standing behind her. Both faces are looking out at the sea. Music: A waltz that turns into a jig.*

Paul   Can you waltz?

Eileen   The priest doesn't approve.

Paul   Damn the priest.

Eileen   Heathen!

Paul   Can you count?

Eileen   I'm not an eejit.

Paul   One, two, three, one, two, three.

Eileen   Here? On Baggot Street?

She holds out her arms. They waltz.

Eileen   Can you do your sevens?

She dances with a coloured handkerchief in one hand.

Paul *looks on with pleasure. He lifts her up and whirls her around. The handkerchief drops.* **Paul** *takes it.*

Act One

Scene One

Dublin, 1935

A bedroom in a poorly furnished house. A man is in the bed. He is in his sixties, thin and dying. Two sons are in the bedroom with him.

Paul *takes out a penny and throws it, catching it on his palm.*

Cecil *flies a paper plane.*

Paul   Let's get it over with. The poor bastard is in agony.

Cecil   What about Ma?

Paul   What about her?

Cecil   Should she be asked?

Paul *tosses the coin. He catches it and covers it with his palm.*

Cecil   We should ask her.

Paul   'Procrastination'. Interesting word. Is it English or Irish?

He uncovers the coin.

Cecil   Bet you sixpence it's Greek.

Paul   Deal.

Cecil   Am I right or am I right?

Paul   Latin.

Cecil   Shite. Ah well, it wasn't a real bet. Not in front of himself.

Paul   That's two bob you owe me. And you're still a dirty procrastinator.

Cecil   Protestants procrastinate passionately at Purim! Now, young doctor, let me ask you something before I beat

you to a pulp. Are you a Protestant Jew or a Catholic Jew?'
Before I beat you in the *pupik*. *Pupik*. Hebrew!

Paul   Polish.

Cecil   Yiddish!

Paul   Polish and Yiddish!

Cecil   Yes! Now I don't owe you sixpence!

Paul   You don't know what it means?

Cecil (*mock professorial*)   *Pupik* is the Jewish term for navel or
the Latin *umbilicus*. Birds don't have an *umbilicis*. And they
don't fall out of trees when they're sleeping. Did you ever
think about that?

Paul   Heads?

Cecil   What's the hurry?

Paul (*parodying the Irish saying*)   Oh sure, when God made
time, didn't he make plenty of it.

Cecil   Sure haven't you got a pretty nurse to see?

Paul   And if I have, what's it to you?

Cecil   Eileen O' Reilly. You want to get in her knickers, is
that it? You think Ma'll let you marry a *shiksa*?[1]

Paul   Tails then.

Cecil *throws a paper plane into the air.*

Cecil   Suppose he can hear us?

He picks up the plane.

Paul   Of course he can bloody hear us. And he's wishing
we'd put him out of his misery now.

Cecil   Tell him about you and Eileen. That'll save us doing
the job.

---

[1] Yiddish for a non-Jewish girl or woman.

Paul   Will you shut up about her.

Cecil   She's a bit of alright that nurse.

Paul   I said shut it.

Cecil *throws the plane again.*

Paul   Will you stop that bloody nonsense.

Cecil *picks up the plane.*

Paul   Will you look at him. Bones sticking out worse than a Friday night chicken. Is that a life worth living?

Cecil   What does the Talmud say?

Paul   Jaysus, who cares what the bloody Talmud says. Yes or no?

Cecil   Suppose we ask him again?

Paul   You *lobbus*.[2] He's been begging for out for the past week.

Cecil   He might not be ready.

Paul   No man is ready to die.

Cecil   Da. Paul wants to marry Eileen. (*He puts his ear to his father's mouth.*) Still breathing. Well, what do you know. You could bring her here. Maybe it would bring him back to life. Doesn't the corpse get a hard-on near the end?

Paul   I'll kill you, you shite.

Cecil   Just like our ma. No sense of humour. You think himself and Ma had fun at all?

Paul   Sure didn't they only do it twice. You and me. He never even liked us.

Cecil   Not true. When we got into medical school. Sitting so proud, like a little Litvak. And you remember how he pulled out three fat Havanas from his pocket. We sat there

---

[2] Yiddish for a lazy person.

smoking. Saying nothing. Like he was Abraham with Isaac and Ishmael.

Paul   Another pair of Jewish *schmucks*.[3]

Cecil   Was Ishmael Jewish?

Paul   Eejit.

Cecil *examines the paper plane.*

Cecil   You know, every night, I dream I am back there taking finals. Sitting, looking at the bloody question, and not knowing the answers. Sweating. Is it an appendix I have to do, or a hernia? I never wanted to be a doctor.

Paul   Jaysus, confession time.

Cecil *sings the melody from Kol Nidre.*

Paul   Well, if it isn't our very own Caruso. They'll be queuing down the street.

Cecil   Ma pushed me into it. (*Imitating his mother.*) 'A chazan doesn't make enough to feed his family.' But it's all I ever wanted to do. Sing in the synagogue. Make people happy, with my voice. Or a pilot.

Paul   And I wanted to be Johnny Weissmuller in *Tarzan*. Well, boyo?

He throws the coin at **Cecil**. **Cecil** *looks at it.*

Cecil   Why is the bloody English monarchy on Free State money?

Paul *snatches back the coin.*

Paul   Make a bloody decision.

Cecil   Heads.

Paul *turns over the coin.*

---

[3] Yiddish for 'fool' or 'dick'.

Paul   Well, what do you know. King George's head says, 'Hello, Jewboy. Time to kill your da.'

He hands over the syringe to **Cecil***.*

Cecil *takes it and prays.*

Cecil   *Shema Yisroel adonai elohainu adonai echad.*[4]

He does not move. **Paul** *in exasperation takes the syringe from his brother and injects his father while* **Cecil** *continues praying.*

Sound of sea.

Scene Two

Killiney Bay

Paul *is walking along the beach at night with* **Eileen***. They are laughing. He kisses her. They sit on a bench in a beach hut. A lighthouse lamp flashes regularly.*

Eileen   Look at the moon. And the sound of the waves. You think everyone is dead and we are the only people in the whole world alive.

Paul   You and me. And not a squirrel or a mouse or a giraffe.

Eileen   A giraffe! Let's ride on his back!

Paul   Where is he?

He runs around and grabs **Eileen***.*

Paul   Here. Oh look he's there. No there!

They kiss. It gets hot. She pulls back.

Paul   What's the matter?

---

[4] Jewish prayer in Hebrew: 'Hear O Israel, the Lord our God, the Lord is One.'

Eileen The lighthouse. The man inside. You think he gets lonely? Perhaps he sees all the dead souls that wander from the shipwrecks all round.

Paul Metempsychsosis.

Eileen What?

Paul Transmigration of the soul. Like the Hindus. Maybe a dybbuk.

Eileen Will you listen to himself showing off. And what in the name of Christ is a dybbuk?

Paul A dybbuk is when someone's living soul goes into the body of another.

Eileen Like yours in mine?

Paul *touches her tenderly.*

Paul Is that what you think?

Eileen Maybe I'm a Jewish baby stolen away by the fairies. That means we are both Jews.

Paul Dance for me . . .

Eileen *does her sevens.*

Paul You're not a Jew.

Eileen And why would a Jew not do her sevens? You're not a real Jew. You're a bloody monster.

Paul (*playing the fool*)   I'm a golem and I'm going to do terrible things to you!

Eileen No I'm going to haunt you even when I'm dead.

She hugs him. He looks out to sea.

Paul Over there. That's England. The Mother Country, I don't think.

Eileen How did your family end up in Dublin? Rum place for a Jew.

Paul   They bought a ticket from the Old Country for the United States. When my grandfather arrived on land, everyone was speaking English. America! The *Goldene Medina*![5] He looks up. 'Where are the skyscrapers?' 'Some Yiddisher bastard bled me dry.'

They kiss. She pulls away

Paul   What's wrong?

Eileen   Nothing.

Paul   You weren't so shy last week, pretty nurse.

Beat.

You worried? Don't be. I'll be careful.

Eileen   Eejit!

Paul   Come closer.

Eileen   Someone might see.

Beat.

My da's been following me.

Paul   What?

Eileen   Since Ma died.

Paul   Six months and you said nothing to me?

Eileen   He knows about us.

Paul   Jaysus.

Eileen   Said he saw us in Bewley's.

Beat.

In Bewley, 'with the filthy Jewman'. He takes his strap /

Paul   / I'll beat the living daylights out of him.

Eileen   He made me promise to stop it.

---
[5] Yiddish for 'golden land'.

Paul No!

Eileen He's my da.

Paul What'll we do?

Eileen You and me /

Paul Yes?

Eileen He'll murder me.

Paul We'll get married. We'll go to England and get married.

Eileen Don't be silly. You've just qualified.

Beat.

And anyway, what will your ma and da say?

Paul My da . . .

Eileen Your da what?

Paul *gets up and looks at the sea.*

Cecil *sings the Hineini.*

Scene Three

Dublin

The synagogue. Light on three men. In shadow are the women in hats – they are either in a separate stage area or raised up. **Paul** *is saying Kaddish for his father.* **Cecil** *is with him. Both are in prayer shawls.* **Paul** *prays in Hebrew and breaks into English. This is what he is thinking while he prays:*

Paul *Yit-ga-dal*[6] . . . (*Thoughts.*) Why is it that the eldest son says Kaddish for his father? If it was the youngest, it would be Cecil and he loves this rigmarole. Who'll say it for me, I wonder? Nobody. I'll drown on a gorgeous cruise in the Mediterranean with a lovely girl and our bodies full of champagne will float off into the horizon.

---

[6] Start of the Aramaic prayer the Kaddish, 'Thy name shall be great'.

Beat.

Goodbye, Da. What sort of bloody life did you have in the end? None at all. Selling holy pictures to the Catholics. Was that a life? England and Ireland. Was that a bloody life? What about the rest of the world? And always the little Yid made scared by his own father. What did you think when your dad beat the Jaysus out of us every Sunday morning because we wouldn't learn Hebrew? 'Now it's your turn, boychick!' Grandfather, *zayde*, such soft words for a man with a strap. Shtetl to Clanbrassil Street, trying to strap the *meschugass*[7] out of his beautiful grandsons. Jaysus, why was I scared of the little whippet of a man with a Yiddish in his Irish – so strong you can choke on it. Yes, Da, I can see you at *zayde*'s funeral. Saying Kaddish like me now. Jaysus. Son and son and son and on and on, the same bloody nonsense. When does it end? I'll make it end. My Eileen's got the creamiest thighs in all Ireland. Apart from Ma, Da, did you ever see a woman naked? Did you ever sit on Killiney Beach and make fast, furious love with a good Catholic girl? No. You married who they said you should. Always did what your da told you. Well, to hell with you, Da! I'm going to marry Catholic Eileen and there's damn all you can do about it. I'll marry Eileen and have *goy*[8] sons. And you know what, Da, I won't even tell them they're Jews.

Scene Four

Dublin

The kitchen. **Minnie** *is preparing food.* **Paul** *enters whistling the waltz. He waltzes with* **Minnie**. *They are having fun. She stops.*

Minnie   You shouldn't whistle. Not for a year.

Paul   A year, is it?

---

[7] Yiddish for 'craziness', or non-conformist behaviour in this context.
[8] Yiddish for gentile.

Minnie   Call your brother down, will you? Dinner's ready.

Paul   In a minute.

Minnie   I don't want it to get cold.

Paul   I've something to tell you.

Minnie   Oh?

Paul   I've met a girl.

Minnie   A girl is it?

Paul   I love her.

Minnie   *Mazel Tov!*[9] A Yiddisher girl? (**Paul** *is silent.*) Don't bring shame, my son.

Paul   Shame?

Minnie   Will you call Cecil or do I have to go upstairs myself?

Paul (*shouting up*)   Grub's up.

Minnie   You didn't answer my question.

Paul   There's no shame in loving someone different.

Minnie   Love is it? Forget love, my boy. It's duty that counts.

I'm selling the house.

Paul   What?

Minnie   I can't keep it on. The mortgage.

Paul   What?

Minnie   I've seen the solicitor.

Paul   What?

Minnie   Your father left debts.

Paul   What debts?

---

[9] Hebrew for 'good luck', or 'congratulations'.

Minnie   Didn't he gamble all over town.

Paul   How much?

Minnie   Two thousand.

Paul   You're pulling my leg.

Minnie   I don't have a sense of humour.

Paul   Two thousand. How?

Minnie (*in the fast style of a sports commentator*)   1921 Ballyheron, 1923 Waygood, 1925 Zionist, 1926 Embargo, 1930 Rockstar, 1934 Patriot King. Will you just listen to those bloody names. This girl /

Paul   Two thousand pounds?

Minnie   What's her name?

Paul   Eileen O'Reilly.

Minnie   That's why I have to sell.

Paul   And where'll we live?

Minnie   England.

Paul   England's the enemy.

Minnie   Will you get that Irish nationalist nonsense out of your thick head.

We take the ferry in ten days.

Paul   Ten days!

Minnie   Your father's cousins will have us. The East End. Just 'til we get settled. It's the least they can do.

Paul   What did you tell them?

Minnie   Everything.

Paul   Our father brings shame on the family and we go *shnorring*[10] to our posh English relatives. I won't have it.

---

[10] Yiddish for 'begging'.

Minnie They're not posh. They've little more than us. You won't have it! There's no choice.

Paul Ten days. Jaysus, Mary and Holy St Joseph.

Minnie Don't talk like that.

Paul Our da? He is our shame.

Minnie I've got a buyer.

Paul Already?

Minnie Mrs Witztum next door. She's another set of twins on the way.

Beat.

Paul You go. With Cecil. I'll follow. Eileen /

Minnie What Eileen? We all go together. You're the *mensch*[11] of the house now.

Paul No!

Minnie Fine. Bring the *shiksa* wife with you. You going to clothe and feed her with what?

Paul I said, I love her.

Minnie (*angrily*)   And I love you.

Paul You never said that to me before.

Minnie You're all I've got.

Paul Just give me time.

Minnie Time? Time? My parents, they got up and they left.

Paul This is not a bloody pogrom.

Minnie The mouth on the boy. 'Honour thy father and mother'. Well, thy mother /

---

[11] German for 'person'; in Yiddish someone who is admirable.

Paul   Go without me.

Minnie   A mother will never leave her son.

Paul   Please!

Minnie   Who sweated to get you and Cecil to medical school? You think it was your da? It was me. That's what love is. Not what's hanging in your sweaty *gatkes*.[12]

Paul   I won't go.

Minnie   I've bought the tickets. You'll work as a junior doctor in the London Hospital. For a year you won't earn much, but after /

Paul   / I am begging you, Ma.

Minnie   The contract's signed. A new family's moving in.

Paul   No!

Minnie   I have the right to sell my own house, don't I?

Paul *is silent.*

Paul   Don't ruin my life.

Minnie   You ruined your own. Behind my back running around with Eileen O'Reilly.

Paul   And what of it?

Minnie   A Jew should marry a Jew.

Sounds of Big Ben before striking.

Scene Five

On the Boat to England

Tight spot on **Minnie** *and* **Paul** *on the boat.* **Cecil** *is in shadow.*

Minnie *holds* **Paul** *from behind. He is silently sobbing.*

---

[12] Yiddish for 'underpants'.

They face out to sea.

Minnie   It's alright, my son. It's alright.

Sounds of Big Ben striking.

Scene Six

The London Hospital, Three Months Later

*The **Ensemble** speaks the following to show the work of the junior doctors:*

Geriatric
Paediatric
Anatomic
Psychotic
Hypochondriac
Bacteria
Bacillus
Barbiturate
Germs
Jugular
Jaundice
Diphtheria
Scarlet fever
Whooping cough
Tuberculosis
Scrub, scrub, scrub
Hydrocephalus
Water on the brain
Sacro iliac
Carcinoma
Cardiovascular
Macular
Mother, help me!
Give me water!
Waters break
Obstetrics

Maternity
Wing
Bird
Luftmensch[13]
Mother
Help me
Help me!
Mother
Birth

Everyone screams.

Cecil *and* **Paul** *are given a child in a bloody cloth.*

Paul   It's a girl.

Baby screams.

Cecil   Never mind what's between her legs. Look at her face.

Matron *takes the baby.*

Matron   Oh hell.

Paul   What do we do?

Baby screams. **Cecil** *holds his ears.*

Matron   Toughen up, Paddy . . . Go and wash it.

Cecil   Here?

Matron   Kitchen. Get a move on.

Paul   Poor bastard.

Matron   Window open.

Baby screams.

Cecil   You sure, missis? It's cold out there.

Matron   Matron not missis. Nice and wide.

Baby screams. **Paul** *takes the child. He kisses it.*

---

[13] In German *Luft* means air and Mensch means a person. The Yiddish expression corresponds to the English description of a man with his air in the clouds.

Scene Seven

London, 1936

A street in the East End. Sound of **Oswald Mosley** *giving a speech.* **Paul** *and* **Cecil** *are standing listening at the side of a crowd who are offstage.*

Mosley   England is not finished. England is not dead. When we have gathered together all men and women of our race, there is nothing that we cannot do.

He raises his arm in a Nazi salute.

Cecil   Will you look at that. Sir Oswald bloody Mosley. (*Posh English accent.*)

'Let's not be defeated by world capitalism. And the Jews.

The communists!

The capitalists!

All Jews!'

He does a prat fall.

'The communists,

The Jews.'

He does a prat fall.

'The communists,

The Jews.

The communists,

The Jews.'

He dances.

'Look out! They are everywhere. On the street corner. In the factory. You will even find a Jewish communist capitalist in your very English cup of tea. Buckingham Palace, in my lady's chamber. Oranges and lemons say the bells of St Clement's. Oranges from Jaffa. A Jewish plot. Even the

Christians are secret Jews!' Jaysus, they make me sick. We should've stayed in dirty Dublin.

Paul   You know what I do when I hear all this English Nazi shite?

Cecil   What?

Paul   I think of something quite gorgeous. Like a lovely female. That's what I do.

Cecil   And where will that get you?

Paul   Don't you know it's the movement that catches the eye. The billowing of a dress in the wind. A certain walk. The head high with a cute little hat, just a bit mysterious and proud, the little firm titties, the shapely waist, the legs high stepping with a neat calf. When I hear that English Mosley shite then I think of the poetry of women.

Cecil   A bitch in heat. *Feh!*

Paul   You know it's awful rum. All day you can be looking at women's bodies in the hospital and you'd think you'd be sick of all that now, but it's not the case is it, the streets are full of women. (*A woman passes.*) Will you take a look at that! Mm . . . What I wouldn't do with her.

Cecil   What happened to your lovely Eileen? Threw her over, did you. You cruel bastard.

Paul   You *mamzer!*[14]

Paul *goes to hit him.* **Cecil** *backs off.*

Cecil   What did I say? What did I say?

Scene Eight

London's East End

Dream sequence. **Paul** *is watching* **Eileen** *Irish dancing. The beating of her feet becomes the beating of a punch bag in a gym.*

---

[14] Yiddish for bastard.

The boxing gym. **Paul** *is working out with a trainer. It is his first time.*

Harry   Stand properly. Up. You got to protect yourself. You're a stand-up boxer, most Jewish boys are. You're far too old for all this but we'll see what's there anyway. Your face. Protect it. Keep the hands up. Lead with your left – what are you, right handed? – so you lead with your left. Come on, kid. Move. Why are you standing back? Don't stand square or you're going nowhere. On the side, keep the feet moving on the side. Bobbing and weaving. No, that's wrong. You've got to keep the elbows in to protect yourself. Keep the concentration there. Now move. I said move, boy! (*He lifts his hands.*) Now stick a left hand. (**Paul** *hits* **Harry**'s *right hand.*) Keep your chin down. (**Paul** *hits again.*) No, don't throw your punch from backwards. Look, I can see you taking your hand back. I know what you're going to do and I get in first. Bang. Throw your punch from where it is. Bang. Bang. Now try landing the left as well as the right. Good. Now we'll try some combination punches. Combination. It's like dancing, a few steps at a time so a few punches at a time. Use the advantage you've created. If you hit the guy, he's stunned. You hit him in the head, then the gut. Or you go head, gut, chin. I told you stop standing back. You never step back. You hit him, he's off balance, you hit him quick again – take the advantage. If you throw one and miss, he'll be ready to counterpunch the boychick, and that you don't want. You need to train boy, you can't box if you don't train. Run, skip, get to that punch ball every day. Be a tough Jew. (*They stop.*)

Paul   Tough Jew. Tough Jew. Tough Jew.

He hits out at **Harry** *who dodges him.*

Scene Nine

London, 1936

Friday night dinner. **Minnie** *is preparing the table.* **Cecil** *throws a paper plane. The others ignore him. She lights candles and says the* *prayer for Sabbath. She covers her head for the prayer and takes off the scarf when it is done. The boys are sitting round with caps on.*

Minnie (*blessing over newly lit candles. Her head is covered with an unfastened scarf*)   *Baruch atah adonai elohainu melech haolam, asher kiddishanu b'mitzvotav, vitzivanu l'chadlik ner shel Shabbat. Shabbat Shalom.*[15]

They kiss each other. **Cecil** *says the blessing for the wine.*

Cecil   *Baruch atah adonai elohainu melech haolam, boreh peri ha-gaffen.*[16]

Paul *says the blessing for the bread.*

Paul   *Barchu atah adonai elohainu melech haolam, hamotzi lechem min ha'aretz.*[17]

Cecil   Ma. Just do the soup. Alright?

Minnie   Are you not well?

Cecil   And keep the chopped liver for breakfast.

Minnie   Whatever you say.

She pours out soup from a tureen.

They drink wine.

Paul   He's sick because of what we have to do.

Minnie   Have to do?

Paul   Some kids come out wrong.

Minnie   Wrong?

Paul   A bad birth. It's there in the eyes.

Minnie   What?

---

[15] Friday night blessing in Hebrew: 'Blessed are You, God, Ruler of the universe, who sanctified us with the commandment of lighting sabbath candles. Welcome to the sabbath.'

[16] 'Praise to You, Lord our God, Sovereign of the universe, Creator of the fruit of the vine.'

[17] 'Blessed are You, Lord our God, King of the universe, who has brought forth bread from the earth.'

Cecil   Matron's orders. 'Leave it on the porcelain sink.' The little girl. No clothes, shivering . . .

Minnie   What?

Cecil   It can last an hour. The sound. I can still hear it.

Paul   The mother never knows. 'Sorry, missis, your baby was born dead.'

Cecil   You think that's right?

Paul   I don't know.

Minnie   Couldn't the child be saved?

Cecil   For a life of misery?

Paul   The kid wouldn't be miserable. It's the mother.

Cecil   But is it right?

Minnie   They used to leave infants on the side of the mountain.

Cecil   Wasn't that the Greeks? All those places with Jewish slaves. The Persians. The Egyptians. And we don't speak any of those languages. What a bloody waste.

Minnie   They should have told the mother the truth.

Paul   Sure she feels sad for a while but she can have another without the burden of the first.

Minnie   I'd've taken her. A girl. I'd've liked a girl.

Paul   Kids like that, they never grow up.

Cecil   Dead by twelve.

Minnie   It's a life. A new life. We have no right.

Paul   Who's going to pay for it?

Minnie   It's murder.

Paul   We are doing it a favour.

Minnie   Did you hear me?

Paul *pours wine.*

Paul (*bitterly*)   *Shabbat shalom* and let's enjoy the bird, shall we?

Minnie *does not move.* **Paul** *and* **Cecil** *exchange a look.*

Cecil   Where's the fowl, Ma?

Minnie *leaves.*

Cecil   I hear Harry Cohen is to be our new father.

Paul   What?

Cecil   She's been seeing a lot of him. Still a looker, why not?

Paul   That's why she hangs around the gym. And I thought she was wanting to watch me.

Cecil   She misses a bit of how's your father.

Paul   / Jaysus.

Cecil   It bothers you?

Paul   Did I say that?

Cecil   It bothers you.

Paul   At her age!

Cecil   So what?

Paul   And Harry Cohen?

Cecil   You're jealous!

Paul   What?

Cecil   Don't spoil it for her.

Paul   Spoil what?

Cecil   She listens to you.

Paul   Let her marry him. Naomi Minnie Green to Mrs Cohen!

Beat.

She stopped me marrying Eileen.

Cecil   I didn't know that.

Paul   I should never have let her.

Cecil   Why didn't you tell me?

Paul   And you'd've done what?

Cecil   Nothing. Will we have to call him 'Da'?

Minnie *enters with the chicken.*

Minnie   What's wrong?

Paul   You getting married, Ma?

Minnie   What?

Paul   To Harry Cohen. Behind my back?

Cecil *throws the paper plane in the air.*

Minnie   What?

Paul   Our father hardly cold and you running round with other men? Is that the truth?

Minnie   I haven't said –

Paul   Waiting for my permission is it?

Minnie   His wife died last year.

Paul   That's convenient then.

Minnie   At least he's not down the bookie's.

Pause.

It's decided.

Paul   Is it now.

Minnie   And he's a Jew.

Paul   Well, that's alright then.

Minnie   Cecil can sing at our wedding.

Paul   And you want me to do what? Dance the hora?

Scene Ten

The London Hospital, 1936

Paul *and* **Cecil** *are taking off their scrubs.*

Paul   When he cut through the bone. With a saw, like he was cutting wood. The sound. The smell. I always expect to see little people inside the skull.

Cecil   Suppose we take out too much?

Paul   And if the cancer comes back /

Cecil   / and they cracked open your skull for nothing at all.

Paul   They say that if you touch one section of the brain, then all your life flashes before you /

Cecil   I saw a photo in a magazine. Lovely, brown Jewish girls smashing stones in a quarry.

Paul   Eileen. Why can't I cut her out of my brain? She taught me to dance.

Cecil   Palestine. Working. In shorts. Those legs! You want to bury your face in them. Gorgeous!

Paul   Jewish girls.

Cecil   Such good-lookers

Paul   I take them out. To dinner. To the films. Clark Gable. Greta Garbo. But when I put my arms around them, I freeze. It's like taking out your sister.

Cecil   We don't have a sister.

Paul *hits at him playfully.*

Cecil   Our cousins, in Palestine. Why don't we go over there and live with them? A kibbutz. Picking oranges. Meet lovely girls. Make babies.

Paul   Are we Zionists?

Cecil   The Irish have a country. The Indians want one. We Jews need one.

Paul   Palestine. 'A land without a people for a people without a land.'

Cecil   But that's not true is it.

Scene Eleven

The Gym, 1936

Paul *is skipping.*

Harry   Your mother and I are getting married.

Paul (*unenthusiastic*)   *Mazel tov.*

Harry   I want your blessing.

Paul *does not respond.*

Harry   You loved your father.

Paul   Did I?

Harry   Didn't you?

Paul   Love? You got up. You went to school. You studied Hebrew. If not, your grandfather beat the living daylights out of you. You learnt the Torah. You learnt to study at the Protestant school on St. Stephen's Green because the Protestants didn't beat you as hard as the Holy Jo's. You learnt to listen when your parents talked of how Cromwell let the Jews into England and when the Catholics cursed Cromwell you kept your mouth shut. You kept your nose clean and your head down. And then, when we got into medical school, smart Yiddisher boys, well, we got on with that too. We got on with studying to please them because didn't they want sons who were doctors? Da told us to keep our heads down, to be clean and upright. We had to behave like a *mensch* because we had nothing but our good name and we had to make it our life's work to keep it good. Not to make mistakes was smart. And if we saw others making mistakes, like our teachers in school, we learned to say nothing because wouldn't they say 'You killed Jesus' or, 'Look at the clever Jewboys, don't they know it all.' I don't know about love, mister. I don't know about fathers and sons. I only know I had a grandfather with no money and no English. I only know he used to drill me in Hebrew when I was three years old. *Aleph*, *bet*, *gimmel*, *dalet*, *hey*. And every time I learnt a new word he gave me a chocolate. And so the Hebrew language has always seemed very sweet to me. I only know I had a father who didn't seem to do much but study Hebrew and sell paintings of the Virgin Mary to those who had the faith. I only know that there was always the Old Country – we carried inside even if we had never been there, and that in that Old Country, somewhere in Russia, or Poland or Lithuania. And there they spoke a language which was and wasn't German. I only know that my father died of stomach cancer and now to please my ma, who doesn't love me, and my da who's dead, I am a doctor and I serve the poor and lance their boils, and tell them they are all right, when I know they will be dead of bad food and bad living, and that tuberculosis kills the poor like flies because they can't afford the sanatorium in the mountains. I don't know if I can ever call you father, mister. I can't love the man I want dead.

Harry *spars with* **Paul**.

Harry   So what you doing all this for?

Paul   Stops me thinking about women.

Harry   Uh?

Paul I get angry.

Harry Angry, son?

Paul I see women having kid after kid /

Harry I'll make her a good husband.

Paul / and nothing to feed them.

Harry I'm only forty-five.

Paul I see men worked to nothing /

Harry I don't care if you don't want me to be a father to you.

Paul / coughing blood.

Harry You're a socialist. Good.

Paul Is that so?

Harry I was in Spain.

Paul I didn't know that.

Harry Lots of Jews fought Franco.

Paul And now you're going to tell me how you suffered and I am supposed to feel sorry for you and let you marry Ma.

Harry I didn't suffer, I bloody loved it.

Paul What?

Harry Yidden from all over. Yidden with a gun in their hands. Yidden smashing Franco's fascists. Snap a man's neck did you?

Paul Not yet.

Harry I don't want to fight with you.

Paul What do you want?

Harry   What does any man want? War and women. Fighting and fucking. That's when you know you're alive.

Paul   I am not dead.

Harry   There's a war coming soon.

Paul   I don't want it.

Harry   You want a woman?

Scene Twelve

Toynbee Hall, London, 1936

Harry *cues* **Rina** *to start her cabaret act. She is dressed as a young male musician in trousers and cap.*

Rina   Brooklyn, 1930. Two Jews Finkel and Schminkel meet in a bar. '*Nu*?' says Schminkel, 'So, Finkel, *wie gehts*?' '*Nicht so shayn*,'[18] says Finkel to Schminkel. 'On doctors last month. you know how much I spent?' 'No,' says Schminkel. 'How much did you spend?' 'Seventy-five dollars,' says Finkel. 'Seventy-five! In one month!'

'*Oy*,' says Schminkel. 'Back in the Old Country, for that kind of geld, you could have been sick for two years!'

Light up on **Minnie**, **Cecil**, **Paul**.

Minnie   This is Rina. She's our distant cousin . . .

Cecil   You're my relative?

Paul   Hello, lovely cousin.

Minnie   Rina is from Lithuania.

Cecil   It's a long way from Tipperary.

He sings.

Paul   Will you stop showing off?

---

[18] Yiddish for 'Well? . . . how's it going?' 'Not so good'.

Cecil I didn't know that Jewish girls dress as men and tell jokes.

Minnie Look at her! I'm *shlepping nachas!*[19]

Rina I am here to raise cash.

Paul What for?

Rina To find money for Yiddish theatre, in the Soviet Union.

Cecil A woman, on her own, it's amazing.

Rina Theatre is not just for men.

Cecil And you're gorgeous!

Paul You're a communist?

Rina Yes.

Paul 'The means justify the ends.'

Rina Wrong way roumd.

Cecil *Lobbus!*

Paul And how is Moscow?

Rina *Shayn.*[20]

Paul And you have enough to eat?

Rina Of course.

Paul I thought there was famine. In the Ukraine /

Rina Anti-communist propaganda.

Paul . . . / that the peasants don't like the collective farms.

Rina The West wants to discredit Stalin.

Minnie I read that women are equal in the Soviet Union. That they all have jobs and kindergarten for the children.

---

[19] Yiddish for 'brimming with pride'.
[20] Yiddish for 'beautiful'.

Rina   Women fly planes.

Cecil   I'll become a woman!

Rina   Women drive tractors.

Paul   You want to drive a tractor, Ma?

Minnie   Down the Mile End Road?

Rina   You should come and see for yourself. There is no state religion. Everyone works. No unemployment.

Minnie   No pogroms?

Rina   This is the Soviet Union. Minorities are safe.

Cecil   The Cossacks used to rip the unborn babies from pregnant women and put a live kitten in their uterus. Then they cut the woman's hands off so she couldn't remove the cat.

Rina   That doesn't happen now.

Paul   So your man, Stalin. That fella. Loves the Jews does he?

Beat.

Minnie   What will you do when you go back?

Rina   Train. My body, my mind.

Paul (*mock Russian accent*)   'Big, strong Russian girl!'

Cecil   Little, lovely Litvak.

Minnie   She's the New Jewish Woman.

Paul   Is that so?

Rina   Who wants to make new theatre for a new country.

Minnie   What makes a good play?

Rina   A death, a birth, a wedding.

Cecil   Girl like you, you should go straight to Hollywood.

Paul   *Shmendrick!*[21] She's a serious actress.

Cecil   Stay here, why don't you. We could do double act.

Rina   Do you act?

Paul   The eejit.

Minnie   In the Soviet Union. How is Yiddish theatre allowed if the Jewish religion is not?

Rina   In the Soviet Union, Yiddish is a national language. Like Armenian or Georgian.

Cecil *pours from a bottle of vodka.*

Minnie   *Spasseeba.*[22]

Cecil   *L'chaim!*[23]

Everyone drinks. **Paul** *clinks his glass against* **Rina***'s.*

Paul   To my future bride.

Cecil   No, she's mine.

Paul *looks at* **Rina***. Everyone looks at* **Paul***. A strange moment of silence.*

Rina   If you want to marry me you have to join the Party. Two strong, young men. Useful.

Cecil   I'm not strong.

Paul   'The end justifies the means.'

Rina   I'm serious.

Cecil   I was never good at joining anything.

Paul   I'll join if it means seeing you. Do you like me?

Rina   *Tak. Tak! Tak!*

Rina *knocks the table three times with her knuckles.*

---

[21] Yiddish for a clueless person.
[22] Russian for 'thank you'.
[23] Hebrew for 'To life!'

Cecil   What's that?

Minnie   Yes in Polish. Don't you know anything?

Rina   Molière's theatre. It signals to the audience that the performance is about to begin.

Cecil (*firing a mock machine gun and 'killing'* **Paul**)   Bang, bang, bang!

Rina   But you must both join the Party. (*Awkward pause.*) We fight together so we don't die together.

Cecil   I'd love to take you out.

Minnie   What stops you?

Cecil (*mocking*)   Blind fear.

Paul   A *nudnik*[24] she doesn't need.

Minnie   David and Moishe are walking down Hackney Road one night when they notice they are being followed by a couple of Moseley thugs. David turns to Moishe and he says, 'We better get out of here. There are two of them and we're alone!'

Rina   'And we're alone!' I love it.

Paul   I thought you didn't have a sense of humour.

Minnie   I don't.

Rina   Isaac is sitting in his room wearing only a top hat when Mendel walks in. 'Why are you sitting here naked?'

'It's alright,' says Isaac. 'Nobody comes to visit.'

'But why the hat?' 'Maybe somebody will come.'

The two women laugh.

Minnie   So which of my *schlemiels*[25] do you like best?

---

[24] Yiddish for 'bore' in this context.
[25] Yiddish for (poor) fool in this context.

Paul   At the end of the night, you have to choose one of us.

Rina   Do I?

Scene Thirteen

The Gym

Paul *is jumping rope.*

Minnie   I brought you some lunch.

Paul   What are you doing here?

Minnie   The wedding is set.

Paul   It's too soon for weddings.

Minnie   The stone is set.

Paul   Don't worry Da won't get out from under it.

Minnie   What does that mean?

Paul   In Harry Cohen's bed, do you think of our da?

She slaps him.

Minnie   Why are you doing this to me?

Paul   You are doing it to yourself.

Minnie   Because of the *shiksa*, is that it?

Paul   She has a name.

Minnie   Eileen O'Reilly. Haven't you done enough mourning?

Paul   She's not dead.

Minnie   It's not what I mean.

Paul   Why is it that you can marry who you want?

Minnie   I'm your mother.

Paul   Then don't dishonour my da.

Minnie   I'm old. I want a last taste of pleasure. You deny me that?

Paul   Too old.

Minnie   I'm a woman.

Paul   And I'm a man.

Minnie   You have your whole life ahead of you.

Paul   You even had the bloody *chutzpah*[26] to set up a *shidduch*[27] with the cousin.

Minnie   You could do worse. She's a beauty.

Paul   So is Eileen.

Minnie   You want Cecil to grab her?

Paul   Let him do what he wants.

Minnie   I saw you when you looked at her. Like lightning.

Paul   You know what, Ma. I'm sick of women and love. Sick of all that mush mush mush. There's no time for that now. There's a war coming. You know what that means?

Minnie   If that's so then we need a bit of happiness to remember when we're dead.

Beat.

The wedding. Will you come?

Scene Fourteen

The Wedding and the Demonstration

Stylised tableau. There is the sound of applause. **Minnie** *marries* **Harry** *under a* chuppah.

---

[26] Yiddish meaning bare-faced cheek.
[27] Yiddish for 'match', or arranged marriage.

Cecil *and* **Rina** *are there.* **Paul** *has his back turned on his mother. He stares out at the audience. He takes out the coloured handkerchief that belonged to* **Eileen***.*

Harry *smashes a glass under his foot. The group clap.*

Paul *throws a glass against a wall.*

Clapping turns to drumming.

Spotlight on **Minnie** *wearing her white wedding veil as all the cast listen to the crowds.*

Voices   We want our country back. England for the English!

Yids out. Go back to Palestine. We'll show the stinking capitalist Jews where to go. Yids out! Yids out! Out! Out! Out!

Scene Fifteen

Cable Street, 4 October 1936

Cecil *sings an Irish rebel song from 1916, 'God Save Ireland'.*

Paul *looks around for* **Mosley**'*s men.* **Jonathan** *enters.*

Jonathan   Get off the street. It's safer at home.

Cecil   We're not frightened.

Jonathan   You want our community to get into trouble?

Cecil   Well, milord, don't you worry your soft English head about that.

Jonathan   Off you go, boyos.

Paul   Hey, fella, let the Board of Deputies keep its nose out of our business.

Jonathan   You think you are the IRA and this is the Black and Tans?

Paul   Bloody English Jews. Licking the king's arse.

Jonathan   Uncle Joe does you no favours, you know.

Cecil   Nor does the Board.

Jonathan   Your friend Karl Marx. Are you aware that he did not like the Jews? Off you go, 'boyos'.

Cecil   You go home, 'comrade'. Or will boyo here give you a bloody nose?

Minnie *runs on.*

Minnie   Look at the police. Must be two hundred of the bastards.

Cecil   You all right, Ma?

Jonathan   Madam. I advise you to take your sons home.

Minnie   Do I know you, lad?

Jonathan   A Jewish mother should be home, with her boys.

Minnie   Home is it. No man tells me what to do.

Cecil   You tell him, Ma.

Jonathan *leaves.*

Spotlight on **Minnie**.

Minnie   All those bobbies. Double, single file. Now they are going into the crowd. They are taking out their truncheons. Would you look at that, they are making a passage for the Blackshirts! The police is looking after them! Would you look at that! And no, the crowd won't let them through. Would you look at them pushing the police back. And . . . yes! The police is giving up. The crowd is pushing forward. They won't let there be a space. They are throwing paving stones. Over there! Isn't there a lorry on its back. And over there another. Bloody marvellous barricades! No! The police is up now. On their horses. And there are our fellas up on the roofs throwing pots and pans and I-don't-know-what down on them. And yes! The horses are falling. Jaysus, it's wonderful. And look, there's Harry! He's beating the hell out of one of the Blackshirts.

Paul   The crowd, throwing marbles on the ground

Cecil   and the horses are going down! Down, down, down! It's beautiful.

Paul   Bloody beautiful. We'll show them, we'll show the bastards that want to kill us that we can fight.

Minnie   That we're not frightened of English bully boys! We'll show them we are tough Jews!

Paul   You think Pearse and Connolly felt like this in 1916 at the Post Office?

Cecil *sings 'The Soldier's Song' followed by 'Bella Ciao'.*

Paul *and* **Cecil** *whirl* **Minnie** *around in victory.*

Scene Sixteen

The London Hospital, December 1939

Cecil *and* **Paul** *after an operation.* **Paul** *is reading a letter.*

Cecil   Love letter?

Paul   Eileen.

Cecil   Oh?

Paul   She's getting married.

Cecil   I didn't know you two were corresponding.

Paul   Dead and gone.

Cecil   I've heard piss-all from Rina.

Paul   You and her /

Cecil   Jealous is it?

Paul   Don't tell me she took my kid brother seriously.

Cecil   My luck! If I sold lamps, the sun would come out at night.

Paul   I could've had her.

Cecil   Is that so?

Paul   Sometimes, when we are cutting through corpses our bloody cousin comes into my head. Rina with her warm flesh and her eyes blazing right through you.

Cecil   You gobshite.

Paul   But you know, fella, she's just the same as everyone else. Blood, piss and shit.

Cecil   Quite the romantic hero.

Paul   I leave the blarney to you.

Cecil   If I could find Rina, could we try to get her into England?

Paul (*mock English accent*)   Well wouldn't that be just dandy. *Luftmensch!*

Cecil   Didn't the English let in ten thousand children?

Paul   And turned away their ma and da.

Cecil   You joining up?

Paul   Are you?

Sound of sirens. Cast look up at the skies as lights dim to blackout.

Act Two

Scene One

Tel Aviv, 1946

To suggest the multiplicity of peoples and histories the **Ensemble** *speak the following:*

York. Toledo. Seville. Tunis. Algiers. Antwerp. Warsaw.

Tak! Tak! Tak!

Wasosz, Lomza, Rutki, Radziłów, Jedwabne, Wizna, Piątnica and Zambrów. Kaunus. Krakow.

Tak! Tak! Tak!

Vilna. Danzig. Gdansk. Vienna. Yelizavetgrad, Kiev. Budapest. Bucharest. Prague.

Tak! Tak! Tak!

Moscow. Shanghai. Dora. Ravensbruck. Treblinka.

Tak! Tak! Tak!

Tak! Tak! Tak!

Tak! Tak! Tak!

Scene Two

Tel Aviv

A street café.

Rina Hello, Cecil.

Cecil *stands and looks at her.*

Rina You don't recognise me?

Cecil Forgive me, the voice yes.

Rina Have I changed so much?

Rina *knocks the table three times with her knuckles*

Cecil   Jaysus. Rina?

Rina   Yes.

Cecil   Here, in Tel Aviv?

Rina   I like Bauhaus.

Cecil   How did you get here?

She does not reply.

What are you drinking?

Rina   Vodka. But there is none.

Cecil   Did you know I was here?

Rina   I heard there was a crazy Irishman in Tel Aviv. Entertaining the British troops.

Cecil   And you knew it was me?

Rina   Or Paul.

Cecil   Are you glad it was me?

He makes to kiss her. She avoids it.

Rina   Ten years.

Cecil   I was in love with you.

He sings the beginning of the Italian anti-fascist song 'Bella Ciao'. **Rina** *does not respond.*

Cecil   Where were you?

Rina   Oh, I was touring Pitchipoi.

Cecil   Where's that?

Rina   Where Jews go and never come back.

Cecil   Pitchipoi?

Rina   Theresienstadt. Buchenwald, Dachau.

Cecil   Oh.

Beat.

Rina   How is Paul?

Cecil   Bastard got a posting near Delhi. Deolali.

Rina   Oh.

Cecil   I wanted to be a pilot, you know. But myopic Yids are useless in a Spitfire. They heard that Paddy can sing for his supper.

Rina   Where are you living?

Cecil   Bloody King George Street. I share a room with a thousand cockroaches and 25 million mosquitos.

Rina   I need somewhere.

Cecil   You can sleep in my bed. I always liked hard floors.

Scene Three

Jaffa

Paul   'There's a one-eyed yellow idol'.

Shoshana   'To the north of Katmandu'. Anyone follow you?

Paul   Not even a lizard. What am I to do?

Shoshana   Walk with me.

She takes his arm.

You like Jaffa?

Paul   I imagined it as an orange grove.

Shoshana   Not a filthy port?

Paul   The Clock Tower, it's just like England. I like that Jeffet Street winds up past the Scottish Missionary School and the French Christian Brothers. A little bit of Europe.

Shoshana   Middle East getting you down?

Paul   I like Irish rain. How long will I wait?

Shoshana   You'll get your orders.

Paul   I am not afraid to die.

Shoshana   No use to us dead.

Paul   I know the British.

Shoshana   You are British.

Paul   Irish.

Shoshana   You could pass.

Paul   They're not all bad.

Shoshana   Yes, but they are all here.

Paul   They'll sicken of it.

Shoshana   They hate the Arabs. They hate the Jews. They love us killing each other. Are you with us?

Paul   I'm here, aren't I?

Shoshana   We need to be sure.

Paul   I keep my word.

Shoshana   And how are you going to feel when you dynamite a barracks full of British soldiers sitting down to roast beef and Yorkshire?

Paul   How should I feel?

Shoshana   They are British. You are British.

Paul   I said Irish.

Shoshana   Pro or anti-Treaty?

Paul   Anti. I'm no sell-out merchant. I'm with Dev, well I was before he arsed up to Hitler.

Shoshana   The Irish don't like 'the Jewman'. Where do you fit in?

Paul   Paddies and Yids . . . We have a common enemy.

Shoshana   But didn't Paddy beat you up for killing Jesus?

Paul   Not communist Paddy.

Shoshana   And you're a communist? Or is that a fellow traveller?

Paul   I believe that every man is equal.

Shoshana   And some are more equal than others?

Paul   It's complicated.

Shoshana   We are not communists.

Paul   Yes but you want the Brits out and you're men of action. That's what I like.

Shoshana   Spoken like a true Englishman.

Paul   Irishman.

Shoshana   The Black and Tans are here you know.

Paul   What? Those bastards?

Shoshana   Criminals are useful to the Brits.

Paul   Why didn't I know that?

Shoshana   Paul Green does not watch. He doesn't listen. You need to sharpen up if you're any use to us. Can we trust you?

Paul   I'm no traitor.

Shoshana   You don't seem to like women.

Paul   Really?

Shoshana   No girlfriend.

Paul   I'm choosy.

Shoshana   You're a good-looking man.

Paul   You like me? I like you.

Shoshana   You have something.

Paul   You like me!

Shoshana   In another place. In another time. Who knows.

Paul   Life is for living, comrade.

Shoshana   I'd love it.

Paul   Tonight?

Shoshana   We don't get involved.

Paul   If the Brits hang me, at least I can think of the last time with a beautiful woman.

Shoshana   There is a space between your brain and your *schlang*.[28] Keep it that way.

Paul   Where did you learn your English?

Shoshana   From the best.

Paul   Oh?

Shoshana   British officers.

Paul *salutes ironically*.

Paul   War and women. What else is there.

Shoshana   And how did you get into Palestine?

Paul   A British Army uniform can be useful sometimes.

Shoshana   You still got it?

Paul   Am I in?

---

[28] Yiddish for 'penis'.

Scene Four

Tel Aviv

A small room. **Rina** *in bed with* **Cecil.**

On a chair is a toy paper plane.

Sound of people shouting. Jeeps passing. **Rina** *is sewing a torn white shirt.*

Cecil   Did you ever go to Jerusalem?

Rina   Not yet.

Cecil   The air's so thick you're afraid to breathe. The Arabs. The Jews. The Christians. I can't bear it.

Rina   Why Palestine?

Cecil   I want to watch the birds migrate to Africa.

Rina   But you don't believe.

Cecil   In birds?

Rina   You know what I mean.

Cecil   Do you?

Rina   I must do something with my life.

Cecil   You should go to Jerusalem.

Rina   Why?

Cecil   To understand.

Rina   What?

Cecil   That we all want what we can never have.

Rina   What can't you have, Cecil?

Cecil *looks at her.*

Cecil   What did they teach you when you learn to be an actress?

Rina   How to breathe.

Cecil *smells her hair.*

Cecil   You know what I'd like to be?

Rina   What?

Cecil   Your right breast. No the left.

Rina   Why not both?

Cecil   No. I want to be all of you. And stand bollock-naked in front of a bloody mirror and admire myself all bloody day long.

Rina   Save your humour for Tommy.

Cecil (*sings*)   'I've got sixpence, lucky, lucky sixpence, I've got sixpence to last me all my life, I've got tuppence to spend and tuppence to lend /

Rina   You don't know me.

Cecil   / and tuppence to send home to my wife.' Be my wife. *Tak! Tak! Tak!*

He knocks the table three times with his knuckles.

What are you sewing?

Rina   Did you know about the princess who made six shirts out of nettles to save her brothers who had been turned into wild birds?

Cecil   I've never heard that one.

Rina   In Pitchy Poi I used to sew in my head. How do you cover fray?

Cecil   I'm no *schneider*.[29]

Rina   Make something strong from something weak.

Cecil *examines the shirt.*

Cecil   Is this for me?

Rina   You don't ask me what I am doing here.

---

[29] Yiddish for 'tailor'.

Cecil   Lehi? Stern? You with Begin?

Rina *does not answer.*

Cecil   You are protecting me, are you?

Rina   If you like.

Cecil   And who protects you?

Rina   I don't need it.

Cecil   Haven't you had enough?

Rina   Why didn't the British bomb Auschwitz? Buchenwald, Dachau?

Cecil   I don't want you in danger.

Rina *laughs.*

Cecil   I can guess . . .

Rina   We need a country.

Cecil   I understand you.

Rina   But you sing to the people you hate.

Cecil   Not hate.

Rina   Why can't you join us? Damn you, Cecil.

Cecil   Those lads. They could be me.

Rina   We are you.

Cecil   And what about the Arabs?

Rina   We'll think about that later.

Cecil   When?

Rina   When a Jew jumps from a burning building and falls on another man in the street, do we blame the Jew?

Cecil   That's one way of putting it.

Rina   *We* are not the intruders.

Cecil   No?

Rina   We were here before the Romans. Before the Christians. Before the Muslims.

Cecil   You believe in the Bible?

Rina   I believe in facts. Why do you do it?

Cecil   What?

Rina   Perform for Tommy?

Cecil   I wanted to be a singer. That's what I do.

Rina   Singing for the British Army?

Cecil   The Brits like my act. The Entertainments National Service Association. ENSA. Did you hear about it. Full of stars. Even me!

Rina   Are you a Jew or bloody King George's lapdog?

Cecil   Be a man. Fight. Is that it?

Rina   The man I marry will be a fighter.

Cecil   Is that so?

Rina   Ben Gurion will take you.

Cecil   Oh, so you think his hands are clean?

Rina   Nobody is clean. *Schmutzig! Schmutzig! Schmutzig!*[30]

Beat.

I was in a block with other young women.

Cecil   I understand.

Rina   Understand? He understands!

She claps wildly. until she is exhausted.

Bravo! Bravo!! Bravo!!!

---

[30] German for 'dirty'.

Cecil   Rina!

Rina   And you want me to worry about the Arabs.

Cecil   They're here because they're here, because they're here.

Rina   Always a joke, a song, anything but action.

Cecil   And in your opinion, what should we do?

Rina   First kick out the British. Then the Arabs.

Cecil   Why? Because God gave us Eretz Israel?

Rina   God died in Auschwitz.

Cecil   We lived with them before.

Rina   Abraham cast out his concubine Hagar. And her son Ishmael.

Cecil   Same father. Family.

Rina   I thought I was an internationalist. Part of the European family. The Jewish communist dream. What a *schmuck*.

Cecil   When the British leave – we share the land.

Rina   The Mufti of Jerusalem loved Hitler. For God's sake, you've got to stand up for your own people, haven't you?

Cecil   Why am I always in the wrong country at the wrong time?

Rina   Stop singing for the British.

Cecil   You make me feel ashamed.

Rina   No Jew should feel that.

Cecil   Ben Gurion wants the state to have Jewish thieves and Jewish prostitutes just like everyone else. I'd like us to do better.

He takes her hand. She allows this for a moment.

I kept failing my exams. And then I qualified. A doctor! Me! Rina. I am not a killer. I am a healer. Can't you love me for that?

Scene Five

Jerusalem street

Rina *walks alone. She is distressed and agitated.* **Paul** *sees her.*

Paul   Rina?

Rina   Yes?

Paul   Rina! It's Paul.

Rina   Paul? 'It's a long way to Tipperary.'

Paul   That was Cecil. I'm Paul. Don't you remember me?

Rina   *Wo sind wir?* (*Remembering a Nazi screaming at her.*) '*Verstunke* Yid!'[31]

She cowers. She laughs. She stops laughing.

Paul   Rina. It's alright. I am here. You are safe.

Rina   Wo?

Paul   Jerusalem. We are both in Jerusalem.

Rina   You are still alive?

Scene Six

Jerusalem, 29 June 1946, Black Sabbath

Enemies:

Rina *and* **Paul** *are on different sides of the stage speaking out to the audience.*

---

[31] German for 'Where am I? . . . Stinkin

Between them is the **British Army Officer**. *The actors speak directly to the audience as if addressing their soldiers. Lines overlap.*

Officer   From Lieutentant General Evelyn H. Barker to all divisional commanders.

Paul   As a member of

Rina   Etzel, I promise

Officer   / His Majesty's Government has authorised the High Commissioner

Paul   to serve the land of Israel

Officer   a declaration of war against the Jewish extremists.

Rina   / to drive out the British

Officer   Convoys with troop carriers and buses to stop at King George V Avenue,

Paul   To create a country /

Officer   Mamillah Road, Keren Hakayemet Street. Search for code books.

Rina   where all Jews can be safe.

Officer   documents, weapons, anything from Haganah, Stern or Irgun.

Paul   Etzel.

Officer   Arrest everyone.

Rina   We fight

Officer   Old men with beards, young girls, as many as you can.

Paul   even to

Rina *and* **Officer**   Death.

Scene Seven

Jerusalem

Planning is all.

Paul   The operation is being undertaken by several of us. But you will not know the whole picture and this is deliberate. Syrian Jews, disguised as Arabs, are going into the hotel to plant the churns with the dynamite. One of the Sudanese hotel staff has sold us his uniform. We'll get some more the same way. We give a warning. No civilians. Only British Army.

Rina   What's my job?

Paul   You'll be given orders.

Rina   We warn the British?

Paul   Yes.

Rina   There are so many Jewish workers in the King David.

Paul   Thirty minutes before the explosion you will call. You will give the warning to evacuate. We don't target civilians. (*To the others.*) You will be divided into two teams; one in the north of the hotel, one in the south. One man in each team will be armed with grenades and pistols; the other will carry matches for lighting the fuses. Gideon will give you the signal. As for the exact date, remain alert, it could be any time now.

They sing Anthem of the Lehi.[32]

Scene Eight

Tel Aviv

Cecil*'s room.*

Rina   Look what I found.

---

[32] https://www.youtube.com/watch?v=1u5Z0GZ1WsE

Cecil   Jaysus, will you look at what the cat dragged in.

Paul   *Shalom.*

Cecil   How did you get here? It's a long road from Mile End.

Paul   First class on the *Queen Mary*, I don't think.

Cecil   *Cead mile failte.*[33]

Paul   *Shalom.*

Cecil   Drink?

Paul   That would be grand. What's it been? A year?

Cecil   I found vodka.

Rina   Where?

Cecil   Wasn't it sitting all lonely in the officers' mess!

He pours for three.

And what's himself doing here?

Paul   Better not ask.

Cecil   Wherever there's shite, you head straight for it.

Paul   And you don't?

Cecil   Didn't we enter this filthy world through the same sweet womb?

L'chaim!

The three raise their glasses. They drink.

Rina   It should be cold.

Paul   I didn't know you two were in touch.

Rina   Yes.

Paul   Since when?

Cecil   A couple of months now.

---

[33] Irish greeting, 'A hundred thousand welcomes'.

Paul   The *ganze mispoche*.[34]

Cecil   Well, on that happy note, will you excuse me? It's nearly the half.

Rina   Does Tommy know you're Jewish?

Cecil   Tommy knows I'm Irish.

Paul   Paddy singing for his supper!

He mockingly sings 'The Wearing of the Green'.

Cecil *leaves.*

Silence.

Paul *picks up a paper plane. He examines it. They stare at one another.*

Paul   Rina, we are soldiers now.

Rina   We are not machines.

Paul *crushes the paper plane.*

Paul   What's this shite with Cecil? You playing both of us now. Are you?

Rina   Cecil was ten years ago. I was a kid.

Paul   I don't get it. You didn't want me back in London.

Rina   I wanted you.

Paul   So why did you take Cecil?

Rina   So I wouldn't get hurt.

Rina   I was wrong.

Paul   You could be caught. You could be tortured. They would make you name names. And they would promise you my life in return. Don't you understand? They hang women, the British.

---

[34] Yiddish for 'whole family'.

Rina   I'm already dead.

Paul   Stay with Cecil and you can both rot in hell.

He kisses her passionately. They have sex.

Scene Nine

Twenty minutes later

Lights up.

Rina   *Anee ohevet ot'h'a.*[35]

Paul   We can't afford to get attached.

Rina   I know you love me from what just happened.

Paul   That's hormones, little Rina. That's spunk. That's mother nature. That's how we're programmed. Like dogs. Love. You think that's love? You really are a naïve little girl. Maybe Cecil loves you. I don't. This is the grown-up world, not fairy tales.

Cecil *walks in.*

Cecil   I forgot my harmonica. Oh.

Paul   Oh, shite.

Cecil   Oh, I see.

Paul   It's nothing.

Cecil   Nothing, is it?

Paul   Not what you think.

Cecil   Aren't I enough for you?

Rina   Cecil.

Cecil   You have to have my brother too?

Paul   I don't want her.

---

[35] Yiddish for 'I love you'.

Cecil   You *shtupped*[36] her and you don't want her? What do you want? You *goniff*.[37] Everything I hold precious you've got to take. To kill. Just like you killed our da.

Paul   How dare you!

Cecil   How dare I?

Paul   I've always bloody loved her. She made me forget Eileen. I just never said.

Cecil   You take. You throw away. You don't care. When Ma wanted a bit of happiness, you couldn't even have the grace to be at her wedding.

Rina   Stop it.

Cecil *doesn't move.* **Paul** *moves around him threateningly.*

Paul   Move, boy. Come on, throw your punch, bang, bang, you got to hit me quick, get those reflexes working, get a blow to the head or to the body, come on, straight to the gut, never step back, you got to get me off balance, not you, reflexes, feet, body, head, bang, bang.

Cecil *hits out violently.* **Paul** *lets him.*

Cecil   You know what? You always had everything. You. Back in Dublin, the girls you wanted, the *shiksas*, the Yiddels, it's Paul, always Paul. What was I? The family *schlemiel*, the *schmuck*. Ma and you. Always Ma and you. The first-born! Me? Did she even see me? You, you got everything. Even when I wanted a toy train, for months I begged for one because all the boys in school they had one and I wanted to be like them and oh yes she bought one with the money our da never made, she went to Grafton Street and she paid good money and who did she give it to? /

Rina   / Stop this. Both of you.

Cecil   / and now he wants to take you.

---

[36] Yiddish for 'fucked'.
[37] Yiddish for 'thief'.

Rina   Take me? Take me? You think I am a prize? I am to
be taken by him? By you? We're here to work. A bloody toy
train. Is this what this is about. What your ma did when you
were pishing your gatkes? Both of you. Get out.

Scene Ten

Tel Aviv

Cecil *is in the street. He is drunk.*

Cecil   Will you love me for what I am, walking down
Clambrassil with the rain pouring down my neck and the
man walking behind me, will he punch me in the back and
don't I want to stand and sing 'til the birds fall from the trees
and dance around my feet Ballymena, Dumdrum will you
drum a bodhran in the Negev, Druse and Muse and Rina
Goldberg Golden Mountain coming down with the rule
book, didn't it take forty years, Golden Calf, Minnie, Manna,
Ma, will you look at that! And didn't lions and tigers walk the
streets of Jerusalem and Abraham knew his servant, the
shiksa, throw her in the desert with her son but the son he
comes back and back and Abraham why did you start all this
bloody nonsense and if you hadn't would there be no bloody
religion but yes there were other gods and it wasn't just you
walking down Clambrassil, little Yiddel with nowhere to go
but to Blarney Land and man kills man, with a knife, with a
blade, cut off the hand, cut off the head, we have no right,
no right at all and can't you just sing and let it go, please
God let it go.

Scene Eleven

Jerusalem, the King David Hotel

Actors make noise with knives and forks. Plates.

*Stage fills with workers at the King David Hotel. Most are dressed as
waiters and waitresses. Some are office workers. Choreographed
movement scene which happens during the monologue.*

Paul   Noon. Everyone is moving slowly. Arab messengers
walk at half speed between offices. There is the sound of
typewriters. Clerks sit and look out of the window, their
brains sleepy from sunlight. The air shimmers in the heat.
The 'Arabs' arrive with the milk churns. In the police station,
there are alarm systems rigged to the main British posts.
Barclays bank. Immigration office. Main post office.
Government house. King David Hotel. Gideon leads the
men into the main corridor. So cool, the concrete floors in
that main kitchen. Doors, passages, offices, frosted glass and,
behind one, a switchboard with women army officers, the
blood system of the military HQ. Oh God, a chef sees them.
What are you doing? Gideon draws his revolver. Avidor
takes out a machine gun. The cooks look up from chopping
the vegetables. What about lunch? It has to be served in an
hour. Monday, the most hectic day of the week. The hotel is
full of Arabs and Jews, Greeks and Armenians, as well as the
British. On the top floor, Golda Meyerson's emissary Harry
Beilin meets Major Ernest Quinn. Quinn liberated Belsen.
Too bad. Quinn is a British officer who likes Jews. Beilin tells
Quinn, stop worrying. All those Jewish arrests. Don't worry.
No retaliation planned. Calm down. The churn has to be
dragged along the basement corridor and past the women
controlling the telephone exchange, past the storeroom and
into the Regence's room. Against the pillars they go. They
are watched only by the Hittite thrones in the room. Out in
the street, the army patrols. Barbed wire, armoured cars
with Bren guns, jeeps. The last churn is being delivered
now. Hell, our man is spotted, there is pandemonium in the
kitchen. An Arab has gone crazy, they say. The British always
blame the Arabs for pilfering. There are five grams of
gelignite inside each cylinder with 50 kilograms of TNT
around it. Sulphuric acid to destroy the wood plug. And
when it drips into the detonator, well, then we'll see, won't
we. There are two real Arab porters hiding under a table. A
Sudanese is bleeding after banging his head trying to escape.
The alarm goes off in the Mamillah Road police station. A
bomb is it? What again? Just relax. It's nothing. Gideon

dressed as a Sudanese leaves and walks out towards Julian's
Way. Amatzia lights a cigarette. With the tip of it, he touches
the fuse. Two hundred yards to the north, Shlomo lights a
cigarette which leads to the four cans of petrol. But the
explosion isn't working. Julian's Way in front of the King
David remains open.

Rina   12:21. I dial Jerusalem 1114. It rings twice.

Ensemble   King David Hotel. Can I help you?

Rina   This is the Hebrew Resistance Movement. We have
placed a bomb in the hotel. The building is going to blow up.
You have been warned.

Ensemble   There are bombs in the hotel.

Ensemble   Who says?

Ensemble   A woman rang.

Rina   Why don't you believe me?

Ensemble   More false alarms.

Ensemble   Shouldn't we evacuate?

Ensemble   A hoax.

Rina   Consulat Géneral de France?

Ensemble   *Je vous écoute.*

Rina   *Nous sommes la résistance hébreu. Nous avons posé une
bombe dans l'hotel King David. Je leur ai dis d'évacuer le bâtiment.
Ouvrez vos fenêtres si vous voulez échapper à l'explosion!*[38]

Ensemble   *Ouvrez les fenêtres!*

Ensemble   *Ouvrez les fenêtres!*

---

[38] Warning given to French consulate:
'I am listening.
. . .
We are the Hebrew Resistance. We have placed a bomb in the King David Hotel. I
have told them to evacuate the building. If you want to escape the blast, open all your
windows.'

Ensemble (*Arab switchboard operator*)   King David Hotel reception.

Ensemble   Bombs. A woman called. Message in Hebrew and English. We should leave.

Ensemble   There's a special table booked for Mr Albana for ten people on Saturday night. Be sure the restaurant gets the message, will you? I'm off to lunch.

Ensemble   Suppose it's for real?

Ensemble   For real? They like to see us standing on the streets. Waiting for explosions that never happen.

Rina (*telephoning*)   Is that the *Palestine Post*?

Ensemble   Yes.

Rina   This is the Hebrew Resistance Movement. We have placed a bomb in the King David Hotel. We have warned them, but they don't listen.

Ensemble   An army officer shot in the basement.

Ensemble   . . . said we'd be killed.

Ensemble   Men in Arab clothes.

Ensemble   Milk cans.

Englishman   Doesn't anyone speak English here?

Arab Woman   We received a call about a bomb. We've got to evacuate.

Englishman   Thank you, but I've heard that one before.

Officer   Best be sure. Go upstairs, everyone. Pull your bed away from the wall and lie on your bed.

Rina   12:32. Only ten people in the bar – usually it's packed at this time.

Ensemble   Bombs in the basement.

Englishman   Well, for Christ's sake, we'd better go and find them.

Englishman   Don't worry. It's another hoax.

Rina   12:37.

Cast speak the following lines:

One   Hot gas, 350 kilograms of TNT.

Sound of explosion. Bright orange lighting effect. The coloured handkerchief flies through the air and lands on the ground.

Two   The pressure is 34,000 times normal.

Three   The clerks on the floor above . . .

Six   Bursting livers, hearts, lungs.

Four   It's a 500 kilogram aerial bomb.

Five   The milk churns have disappeared.

Six   The pillars of the Regence have disappeared.

Seven   The stone walls billow out and seem to dance slowly as they shudder inwards, to meet smoke and flames.

One   Oh, the suction.

Three   Rings are ripped from fingers.

Two   Trees are ripped from the ground.

Seven   Bodies ripped from gravity to fly through the air.

Six   Concrete rip out into the air at a hundred miles an hour.

Five   Arabs in a bus killed outright.

Four   12:37. Thirteen people alive disappear.

Two   Cufflinks, bracelets, wallets, explode into dust.

Three   A Jewish typist's face tears off.

One   It is painted on the pavement below.

Four   Furnace heat, air and dust. I am choking to death.

Five   The noise. It breaks my eardrums.

Six   Girders fall.

Seven   Plaster.

One   Chandeliers and stone snapping necks.

Three   Coat racks piercing chests.

Four   Ceiling fans decapitating those on lower floor.

Five   Pillars dance.

Two   Walls crack.

Six   The noon sun disappears.

One (*ecstatic*)   Oh God, I am alive!

Two   But who do I know is in there?

Three   Look, there are parachutes flying.

Five   No. They are women, their dresses like clouds.

Six   British, Arab, Armenian, Jew.

Seven   Who did it?

Two   How many?

Three   There's a great bloody hole in the King David!

Four   It's the Secretariat that's gone up.

Five   Who is still there?

Six   In the rubble?

Seven   The blond soldier's head crushed under stone.

One   The place looks like a torpedoed ship chest.

Three   Mrs Grey-Donald crawls out.

One   'I'm perfectly all right, my dear.'

Two   The Arab with a squint –

Three   – is straight-eyed now.

Four   His curls are standing on end.

One   Curfew, curfew in thirty minutes!

Five   Arabs and army engineers jacking into the rubble with pickaxes.

Six   Who is down there?

Seven   Quick, doctor, give a shot of morphine to the man trapped below.

Rina   There's a man down there! Get him out.

Cecil *is dead.* **Rina** *sees his ghost. Lighting change. Everyone else freezes.*

Scene Twelve

Rina *isolated in a spotlight. This is a memory scene.* **Cecil** *is dancing with* **Rina**.

Rina   And I am bone-tired. You on me, in me, sucking, devouring me, not letting me sleep as if tomorrow they will kill us and now you must drink me until you have swallowed me and I have totally disappeared.

You suck the saliva out of my mouth like champagne. You ask me to eat something and then pass it to your mouth. I am bone-tired from your body and my eyes – I can't close. Your brother does not love like you. Takes me quickly, urgently, and then it is over, whereas you, as soon as you have emptied you say, let me stay in you, and we remain like that until you start again, caressing gently at first. You want to stay there forever. Your body says if I leave you I will die.

Two brothers. From the same womb and to the same womb. How can two brothers be so different?

Beat.

From one to the other. From you to him. I am Holy Land. (*Laughs.*) The Jews when they left Germany they put soil in their pockets. What does it mean to love the land that much?

The group unfreeze.

One   Get that man out!

Two   His leg is over there.

Three   Is there anything that can identify him? Dog tag?

Four   What's this?

Two   A toy bloody aeroplane

Rina *walks up to them and looks at the plane. She howls.*

Scene Thirteen

Jerusalem, 1947

Sounds of jeeps leaving Jerusalem. Scene opens halfway through a fight.

Rina   We should never have done it.

Paul   You knew what you were doing.

Rina   I thought I died in Buchenwald, I thought nothing would affect me.

Paul   He's living in Tel Aviv. What the hell was he doing in Jerusalem?

Rina   We killed him.

Paul   For God's sake, it was bad luck.

Beat.

Rina   We destroyed the King David. David. Our greatest king. We'll never be able to rule ourselves after this.

Paul   David killed the *schmuck* Goliath if you remember. And we just got Goliath to go home.

Rina   We're forgetting Cecil. Perhaps you killed him because he loved me?

Paul   Why would I kill my own brother. I'd've told him to get the hell out of bloody Jerusalem. You don't believe me. You think that?

Rina   There were other Jews killed too.

Rina   And British and Arabs.

Beat.

Just a mess of bloody flesh. Who cares what they are.

Paul   It's over.

Rina   Is it?

Paul   The Brits are leaving? We won.

Rina   Did we?

Beat.

Paul   What happened to you in the camps?

Beat.

Rina   Nothing.

Paul   I don't believe you.

Rina   Then don't.

Paul   You can't tell me?

Rina (*defiantly*)   Women. They picked the best-looking.

Paul   Oh, God. Rina.

Rina   I am dead. Do you know that.

Silence.

Paul   Why did you take up with Cecil then if you're dead?

Rina   I was curious

Paul   Oh?

Rina   To have a man do it 'with love'.

Beat.

Did you ever love?

A strain from the waltz **Paul** *danced with* **Eileen** *is heard.*

Paul   Can you dance, Rina?

Rina *laughs hysterically.*

Rina   All this killing and he's talking of dancing!

Paul   Did you ever really love someone?

Rina   Yes.

Paul   Who?

Rina   Are you jealous?

Paul   What's his name?

Rina   I don't know.

Paul   Yes of course I'm bloody jealous. I want to kill him. Who is he?

Rina   In the Vilna Ghetto a man gave me his soup.

Silence.

Paul   And me?

Rina   Perhaps.

Paul *smiles.*

Paul   And now you feel guilty.

Rina   To make him happy, I would have married Cecil, and so, as his widow, you, as the brother must take me on.

Paul   Where did you learn that shite?

Rina   That's what you have to do. Marry me.

Beat.

No?

Paul You're Cecil's.

She takes off his shoe and spits on the ground.

What the hell are you doing?

Rina That's what has to be done. Now you are free of me.

Paul How do you know all this?

Rina I am a Jew.

Paul It is the man that spits. Not the woman.

Rina So spit.

Paul No!

Rina Then we must marry. it's the law.

He takes back his shoe.

Paul The law! Thou shalt not kill! That's the law. He once asked me if birds fell out of trees when they sleep. Birds here. They never sleep.

Rina What do we do?

Paul Live in Israel?

Rina We're pariahs.

Paul Live in London?

Rina Enemy country?

Paul That war is over.

Rina Is it?

Beat.

Paul Rina. We could have a child. A boy. We'll call him Cecil.

Epilogue

Light on **Cecil**.

He whistles 'I've got sixpence . . .'

He knocks the table three times with his knuckles.

Cecil   *Tak! Tak! Tak!*

Full cast arrive.

Rina *wears a white veil. She stands with* **Paul** *as if in marriage.*

Suddenly, she turns her head to the side as if seeing a ghost. **Cecil** *stands beside her so that she the bride is between the two brothers.*

Paul *does not see* **Cecil**.

Cecil *sings 'I've got sixpence'. It increases in volume.*

Paul *recites Kaddish with increasing speed as the muezzin's call starts faintly.*

The ensemble stamp their feet. **Rina** *tears at her veil as the sound intensifies.*

Lights fade down to blackout.